RIBS

poems by

Margaret Barkley

Finishing Line Press
Georgetown, Kentucky

RIBS

There are 24 ribs in the human body

ACKNOWLEDGMENTS

Thank you to Les Bernstein and Fran Claggett-Holland and everyone in the Blue Moon Salon for helping me be a better writer and making me believe I could do this.

Thank you to my support posse – Sara Tickler, Jan Brady, Sheryllyn Dougherty, Christina Amri, and Skye Blaine. You held the back of my bike seat when I needed to get my balance.

And thank you to my husband Bud Martin, who supports me always and in all ways.

Publisher: Leah Huete de Maines
Editor: Christen Kincaid
Cover Art: Jan Brady
Author Photo: Dawn Heumann
Cover Design: Elizabeth Maines McCleavy

Order online: www.finishinglinepress.com
also available on amazon.com

Author inquiries and mail orders:
Finishing Line Press
PO Box 1626
Georgetown, Kentucky 40324
USA

Table of Contents

Ribs..1

Live As Though You Are Light..2

Warm Eyes..3

How To Find Out Who You Are, in 3 Parts...................5

Dust Bin..6

What Is There...7

Her Time...8

The Joy Alone...9

Life Game 11

Personal Effects...12

Feeling Him Close...14

Damp Tissue 16

Impermanence...17

The Last Peach 19

Untangling..20

Junkyard Dog...22

Heart Map...25

Unanimous Decision 27

When Mrs. Goodman Said Yes......................................28

Risk Management...29

Slanted Morning Light..30

Secret Pleasures...31

Like A Song..33

I Will Listen..35

Ribs

Flying down the road to town
my mind already there,
I slow suddenly,
shocked into the present
by a perfect set of ribs
jutting up in the middle of my lane
gleaming wet and red in the morning sun
with the tan fur of the body
splayed out flat beneath.

A young deer,
must have been hit in the night.
Already picked by vultures,
this red cage so exposed
I can't turn away
and in that sunlit vision
of small bones
I feel my own ribs picked clean,

my own heart beating
inside its cage
as wet and red as this –
bones arrayed as fingers
of two skeletal hands cupped
to hold precious the center muscle
so loyal to me,
driving blood a thousand miles
through my body.

In one drive-by moment
I am the same as any bony mammal,
the same as you –
fragile and moist,
flesh and blood and breath
held by bone
held by some grace we cannot see
held by time given
till bone exposed again.

Live as though you are light

Are you a being of light now inhabiting flesh?
or are you a series of chemical reactions
causing muscle to move?

All of us are pieces of meat
made living –

Your body, my body, the body of the cat
walking by with her tail alert

Either everything is holy,
or nothing is holy

Quick – which is it?

Either way, your body will someday wear
the face that reminds us of you, but isn't

Warm Eyes

Forgive me if I've told you this before
I tend to do that.
I was born into this world,
then everything wonderful and sad

just happened,
and now I tell the same stories
in different ways, over and over.
You probably do this, too.

We are trying to make sense of this.

When my grandson saw a family photo
without his little sister in it
his mom told him she wasn't born yet
and he asked
"well, where was she?"

and that is exactly the thing I'd like to know.
Where were you before you were born?
Where was I? And how did we end up here?

What luck, to live and breathe in this place
on this blue and green planet,
given sun and trees waving in the breeze,
shameless peonies and roses,
bodies that move and see and feel loveliness.

We really don't have anything to complain about.
Except we do, because
everything hurts.
The wilting, the dying, the losing, the insults of the body,
the knowing that we are here for a blink,
and the not-knowing where we will be after we leave.

I would just like to know how to make the best of it
wouldn't you?
So I'll tell you my stories,
you tell me yours,
and we will listen to each other with warm eyes.

How to Find Out Who You Are, in 3 parts

1.   See the storm coming
        Build a boat
        Put everything you think you
        need to protect
        on the boat
        Sink it
        in the rising water
        that you have imagined,
        and walk away

2.   Dress up as the person
        you think you were born
        to be if only you hadn't
        failed in some way
        Dress in an outfit that is
        perfectly accessorized
        Become a puppet
        operated by a remote
        control device
        held in
        your true hand
        as you sit naked and smiling
        until you are no longer amused
        watching your perfectly dressed self
        Then go do something else

3.   Imagine the world just how you want it
        Notice the world the way that it is
        Become the painter, the canvas,
        the little person in the painting,
        the boat, the water, the sun reflecting,
        the paint sqwooging between fingers
        Become the paint mess on the floor
        the failed paintings hidden
        Become the beautiful stranger
        gazing at the painting hung on the gallery wall
        with flutter of recognition
        time-stilled and silent

Dust Bin

There they are –
sweepings from another day
haircut clippings
used prayers
chips of broken glass and your mother's
best Spode china
police reports
mild regrets
and wrenching grief

When you cut your losses and walk away,
what falls to the floor?
There is no rug to sweep it under
no way to leave it behind,
like we'd hoped

Like a wake behind us
like clattering cans tied to the honeymoon car,
we move ahead, and our discards follow,
sulking, glittering

until one day
we sigh,
tired of our own incessant striving
and turn to face
what has become
a glorious vanguard
behind us, proclaiming
Yes, we have lived

What Is There

This morning I found hopelessness
curled up under my right rib
black and amphibious
firm against me, a slick leech
been there so long
I thought it was bone.

I don't know how I let it in
past the joy in my life,
but there it was.
I reached for it
and the black thing hissed
that times are hard
for everyone
with the economy and all,
what do you expect?

But I worked it loose
pulling against the glue of
disappointment
that held it there
until it draped
long and heavy over my hand
and I let it go.

I don't know what is there instead
up against the crescent of my rib –
not light, but another kind of dark
soft like purple felt
iridescent like night so black
that my eyes imagine the light.
I might even hear singing,
but I don't know yet
where the sound is coming from.

Her Time

She was born
under the belly of the sun,

which explains a few things.

She was born at that time
when the tilt of the planet
makes us all lean away from the light,

when, whether we like it or not,
the quiet voice of darkness calls us in.

She was born when the trees are bare in the cold,
and anything alive is hiding,
or should be.

She doesn't mind waiting,
like the winter fox with taut muscles
at the edge of a rabbit's hole,

or the bear,
curled up in the dark, slowed
almost to death.

She is not afraid of the hidden things.
She reaches into the deep folds of darkness,
lets its skeletal hand point the way for her.

She knows the dances of bone and earth,
the crystalline visions that come from eyes
grown used to the night.

She carries this all year long,
but this is the time
when we must go with her.

She knows the way.
This is her time.

The Joy Alone

In our prayers we ask –
Help me to be more open.
Let me love and be loved.
May I find inner peace.
– and we mean it,
we really do.

Here's what we would ask if we
knew better what we were
getting ourselves into:

Please help me to survive the opening.
Let me learn to walk around
with a broken heart.
May I remember to breathe
in the midst of mayhem and hatred.

For in the asking we will be given.
We will be broken over god's knee
like kindling too long for the fire.
We will ache to be touched and loved.
We will love another, precious and fine,
and be powerless to save them from suffering.

We will be opened,
and when we are
the joy alone could kill us,
and terror and grief are reasonable
companions
as we feel the truth of our predicament.

We are here together
in glory, in grace –
Alive, alive, alive!
What beauty in the green hills,
in your touch on my skin,
in the shining eyes of a child

and there is *no* bargaining here –
to drink from this cup
we must choose to live
with the intolerable knowing
that children die by our hands

that lovers will leave us, somehow
that loss and death and helplessness
are walking with us always,
held by the same glory, the same grace –
Alive, alive, alive.

Life Game

Start with a full tool box,
a skin bag –
arms, legs,
an assortment of organs.

Like a board game –
most players are given
a full set,
then we roll the dice
move around the board,
repeating our turns for as many years
as the game gives us,
surrendering game pieces as we go.
Smaller ones go first,
like wisdom teeth
or flexibility first thing in the morning,
and eventually the bigger pieces go too.
Some players pull the Alzheimer's card
and lose their minds first,
some an arm or a kidney
and some are still playing after the paralysis card
leaves them only blinking eyes to communicate.

And the instructions
inside the box lid
are not complete –
they don't tell us
why we are playing or
what it takes to win.

Personal Effects

You may not want to think about this,
but I'm telling you anyway –
After you die,
someone else will wear your shoes.
Your body will turn into something else
air or leaf mold or forest loam
but all of your things –
the belongings you've collected carefully
or accidentally –

things you use every day
that make your life look like yours,
will be redistributed.
If they're lucky, it won't be to the dump.

Your favorite pen, your dishtowels,
the mess on your desk,
specific personal files with labels,
your underwear, even the ragged ones,
tire gauge, blender,
carefully coordinated throw pillows
and the stretched out sweats you always wear –

People will go through your rooms
trying on your clothes and old hats,
incredulous at your disorganization
or wondering what possessed you to keep *that* thing.

She will pick a vase and a leather jacket,
he will want your ratchet set and
they will give all of your shoes
to the woman with narrow feet
and fill boxes and bags for charity.

People will cry over it,
tell stories about you, what they loved
and the quirks that drove them crazy,
and then, like a flock of birds surprised into flight,
your things will swirl
to land in new places
and something else will be
what's left of you.

Feeling Him Close

Death slouched outside my
window last night,
leaning against the wall
acting as if he had all the time in the world.

All night I felt him there
as I floated at the top layer of sleep
with my hand on my beloved's broad chest.
I wasn't afraid that he was coming for us.
I knew that he just wanted me to feel him close.

Some of the people he visits, he walks right in
and sits at their supper table
so they can smell his breath
real close up.

Last night death loitered by my house,
but he didn't come in, and I was glad
he wouldn't be getting in bed with us
just yet.
Somehow I knew that much.

My friend thought she knew that, too,
and then one day he showed up in a scan of her body,
all of a sudden.
Now she doesn't seem to mind
that he drapes himself on her sofa
or that he likes to stroke her hair.
She made friends with him right away,
and though they are an odd couple,
her looking so healthy and all,
we are getting used to their relationship.

She is actually glowing,
and the more he hangs around,
the more we can accept his good points
like one of those handsome bad boys with a heart of gold,
the ones that take you in a fast car
to places you never thought you could go.

He might decide he wants to take her away
which would break our hearts,
but she smiles and tells us that
it's only a matter of time –
he will take us all.

Damp Tissue

I'm not strong
or wise
or pretty –

I am small and red-nosed and disheveled
and there's no one to blame
and nowhere to go.

Skin is such a fragile container–
maybe if I hold still
I won't spill over
onto the expensive carpet

maybe my wild head
will be camouflaged
against the flowered wallpaper.

I am sitting with my shoes together
waiting for my date to arrive
wringing the damp tissue in my hands.

Give me something to work with,
anything at all.
I am lost and blotchy and embarrassed,
missing the grownup woman

who can smile at a whole room.
I don't know where she went
and I am left with this awkward girl
who doesn't know where she belongs.

Impermanence

The crowd sits in rows of folding chairs
attentive and earnest
while the spiritual teacher
speaks modestly

about the essential nature of reality,
about the part of us which has
always been here and doesn't die,
about the illusion of form –

and I look around at everyone listening
and have a sudden urge
to run my fingers
through each person's hair,
to stroke the soft cheeks
turned toward the stage,
to love them all
in these lumpy human forms,
right now.

Maybe my religion is
a love affair with illusion –
so be it.
Maybe if I sacrifice this life
in the only fire there is,
then I can love it even more.

We all know of impermanence,
that the price of admission here
is that we will lose it all –
how can we bear both the beauty
and the loss?

I must have chosen
once, naively, to bear it.
I must have known, somehow,
that it would be worth it to feel
the sacrifice that loving
always is,

that if I could let my heart break
and then leave it that way,
ecstasy and grief, which were
really never separate,
would find each other again.

I must have been hungry
for the exquisite simplicity of form –
fingers through hair,
your eyes meeting mine,
the treasure of a day,
just one more day here
under blue sky.

I must have known that in the end,
my losses would be strung
one after another
like Christmas lights
leading me home.

The Last Peach

As I cut it into my cereal
holding its round velvet
weight in my hand
I know this could be the
last peach I taste this season –
a few bruises to cut out
the pit loose and cracked-open ready
to grow –
I take a bite right off the knife
and taste explodes in my wet mouth

the last time we make love
we don't know
it's the last
till later

the last peach
the last time
my last day in this body
could be today

I can pretend
I will always have peaches
my lover will never stop wanting me
this life will go on
day after day
whether I notice it or not

but it is the element of surprise,
the remembering that the surprise
will come
that keeps me sharp in my loving
so that I taste this peach, this day,
as if it were my last
feeling joy and the taste of peaches
and the ache of change and loss
all at once

Untangling

My people made beauty with string
grandmas, aunts, all the way back –
pillowcases embroidered and edged with crochet
tea towels and tablecloths stitched with strawberries and daisies
doilies and bedspreads tatted or crocheted thread by tiny thread

My English grandmother cut small circles
from the unworn margins of bedsheets and
crocheted lacy edges to make coasters,
all while raising six children on a Wyoming ranch –
they still work just fine as a perch for my tea

I carried the legacy, as a young mountain girl
embroidering flowers on my overalls
my peasant blouses

Now, needing floss for a project
I bring out my inheritance –
Huntley & Palmer's Assorted Biscuits tin, white with red roses,
Garcia y Vega cigar box from my grandfather
fruitcake tin with the cowboy Christmas scene, his lasso raised –
all stuffed with embroidery floss in rainbow confusion

Before I know it, I am sorting by color
pulling at the tangle thread by thread
like unbuilding a nest
made by time and heritage

Did you know that if you pull at tangled thread
the knot just gets tighter?
Like opposing opinions,
the more stubborn we hold, the more intractable the snarl

I tease another impossible mass apart gently
till it gives way to loose strands –
what would happen if we were
like this with each other,
listening with patience, looking for openings?

Sometimes the knot is already tight,
and I need the dull end of a needle to
encourage release –
the sharp point would only cause more chaos,
like a harsh remark in a conversation

I think about my line of women,
on the prairie with their red necked men,
men on horses and tractors
who shouldered into the job
indomitable in most things –
politics, a stubborn stump, a downed cow,

while the women, strong in their own way,
stood firm against the prairie wind
mending disputes
and fences,
clothes on the line, dough rising

soothed babies and baby chicks,
picked flowers for the table, set with silver
and an embroidered cloth,
sat with other women,
hands and needles moving
weaving community while they were at it

I think about now, in a world tangled
by our own making –
maybe the women can find a way to
tease apart what seems impossible
to some kind of softening
can make beauty
from all of the colors

Junkyard Dog

Let's say, for the sake of discussion,
that before you were born you were made of light,
or something like it.
Let's say that you were not anything at all
like this oddly shaped living thing
(no offense)
that you are now,

but that something of you existed.
Maybe you were just more see-through
or more vast, or fluffier,
but there you were
then in one excited wet moment
the body you know
began, grew for nine months, and landed here.

It was the luck of the draw exactly where –
probably not onto towels on a dirt floor, for example.
My guess is that you arrived in a well-lit sterile room,
probably naked for just a second,
and then you began collecting things,
because that's what we do.

And now here you are –
here we are together in these bodies,
living in a culture *filled* with things,
in a country where the people in charge
are like dumb
drooling junkyard dogs,
protecting their piles of metal and drums of oil,
even sending some of us
to faraway places to do their bullying for them.

We don't know how to be with this
but do the best we can,
collecting things – food, clothes and houses
electronic devices and to-do lists,
earning money to collect more things, and
trying to have a good time in the process.

Meanwhile,
we start to feel a wee bit protective,
like junkyard dogs ourselves, even,
guarding the piles of stuff that we've gathered,
taking things a little too personally sometimes

and lunging at the fence
we've built around all of it.
It's all so much that sometimes
we have to hire insurance people
and attorneys to help.

But here's the great thing –
in the middle of all of this
collecting and protecting
we seem to have been granted,
most of the time,
the ability to learn
and to feel

and to notice what was here all along,
like sunsets
wild-ass fields of orange poppies
and the fact that having a body
is actually quite wonderful
especially when we're
rubbing them around on each other,
or dancing.

We discover that loving someone else
feels better than anything,
and that the important stuff
can't be collected at all.

Somewhere along the way,
there is that tin man moment,
when you know you have a heart
because it's breaking

and you realize that courage is nothing
like a slavering fanged dog –
courage is being willing to let go,
open the damn gate
and share the goods.

If you're lucky,
by the time you're old you've found humility,
which doesn't mean that you're unimportant,
it means that you're *everything* –
because we're all made out of the same stuff,
some kind of light,
something vast and fluffy
covered in skin.

Heart Map

My aching heart
is no poster child,
buys no billboard space,
is still wearing her robe
when company comes,
will not come down to dinner,
wants presents for every holiday
and then some

She is the awkward
guardian of the treasure
She can melt you with a smile,
and then for no reason
flounce onto her bed
and sulk for the whole afternoon

She is simple
but not easy
Given small gestures of love
she will swoon and forgive
everything,
but ultimately
her longing is for the sublime –
your offerings will always
be only temporary measures
But never mind that – give her flowers,
kiss her till her knees give way,
hold her when nothing else will work

Listen, what the songs say is true
My heart wants to be courted,
wooed,
asked out on dates,
knows what she wants
but might be afraid to ask,
breaks open every other minute,
loves you completely,
accepts you more than you imagine
as you sit baffled by her tears

Are you brave enough to
look through her yearning,
cleverly disguised as discontent,
directly into her wide eyes
and love her

Unanimous Decision

the trail is muddy through oak woods
my mind in its own winter
at least I'm out of the house

leaving the trees a meadow opens
a vista of grays
sand-colored grasses
slate sky
clouds of bare branches
everything faded and quiet
I am the same

then, a flicker
just the possibility of color
on a nearing tree

suddenly alert
I see a haze of soft hues
golden and ruby tips
on every reaching twig
on every kind of tree

now all I can see is vibrance
the blackberry vines
draped in rust and ochre
hopeful greens poking through dead grass

the skeletons of last year's
Queen Anne's Lace
sunbursts floating on silvery stalks
bobbing in the breeze
whispering –
spring will come

When Mrs. Goodman Said Yes

When Mrs. Goodman said yes
and opened herself to him

When he came in the door
after work and set down his lunchbox

When he wanted her,
not with wooden groping
but saying "Oh, my Sadie, my Sadie"
and she felt his thick hand
behind her waist pulling her to him

When Mrs. Goodman said yes
and her sensible shoes, her dress
and baking apron
were heaped on the floor by the bed,
his overalls flung

When puffs of flour floated
in the shaft of sunset light through
the bedroom window
and she breathed in his smell
of oil and man

She thought to herself,
"Now supper can just wait"

Risk Management

Once I stored the broom next to the water heater,
a stray straw ignited, and fire
burned away the corner of the kitchen

Life is like that
Another time flood waters filled my house
after heavy rains and high tide
leaving piles of wet ruin

I loved and lost and lost again,
and my broken-hearted gnashing
made another kind of flood
There are no guarantees

I could leave you and take half your money
You could become tight-fisted, boring, or fat
I could nag you about every little thing
You could leave me homeless

While our minds are busy calculating
return-on-investment and risk ratios,
my heart says yes
and bets everything
on the horse with the kind eyes

Slanted Morning Light

The cows are steaming,
the dark lumps of their bodies
lie scattered in the field
in the slanted morning light.
Like a column, fog rises
from each black heap of cow.

And above the small pasture pond, too –
the misty air is fat and gray, suspended.

Another wet cloud floats near the barn.
The hills are soft and quiet, but
the earth must have been up to something
all night long

for her breath
to be so hot and wet
this morning.

Secret Pleasures

Spring is pouring over everything
Unrepentant,
wearing colors much too bright
for any other kind of party

Everywhere you look
there are show-offs –

The cow nudging her still-wet calf to walk
unsteadily in a field of bright yellow
mustard

Red-winged blackbirds swooping and
looping from fence post to tree

Hills vivid and extravagant in green
Horses belly deep in grass

And the light itself somehow brighter,
unfiltered, unabashed

The smells of flowers and green shoots and new
air all competing
blending
inside of me
enough to make me moan

If you listen you will hear
the heavy breathing of the earth
herself –
beads of dampness have collected
on her huge inner thighs,
opened

Her sap has risen
And mine
And yours

Spring has spilled over everything

In towns you will see it too –
New skin is everywhere
Breasts are blooming
People smiling with secret pleasures
are tempted to share them with you

Like a Song

We're all in this together
Peas in a pod
Birds of a feather
Stranded at sea
on a ship we're outgrowing
with our clever self-preservation

We are in this together
neighbors by necessity
in this our only village
Your laundry blocks my view
His music is too loud
When I was sick she brought me soup
and sat with my baby all day
We all worry if anyone gets a cough

We grow our vegetables
in the same dirt
fed by leavings from my kitchen and yours
The trash pile at the edge
of town is getting too big to manage
and the old man stumbles home
drunk late at night, just like
he did when he was younger

We are this together –
infinite light
formed into seemingly separate
gatherings of molecules
that look like flesh
Digestive systems with
feet to carry them
Remarkable circuitry hungry for life

Hearts longing for
an interconnectedness
we almost remember,
finding it for moments
in each other's arms
Hearing it like a song
the wind carries
at the edge of the known forest

I Will Listen

to you ramble on
about what you did, and what you
need to do, how your work is going,
who does your hair and
what you had for dinner

just to get to
the heart of it
the thing that makes you sing
and crow
or wail
and writhe –
the story that haunts you
when no one is looking
the memory that mists your eyes
the longing that could kill
you all by itself.

I will wade through used tissues
I will offer up my body to be misted with gossip
I will laugh at your jokes
I will hold a sign that says I will work for food
and wait a hundred years
until you look me in the eye
and tell me something real

Margaret **Barkley** lives in Sebastopol, California with her husband and has a vibrant extended family of adult children and grandkids. She is from Wyoming and has roots there that go back several generations. Its open spaces and beauty imprinted a love of nature and adventure, and she continues to explore wildness wherever she is.

Margaret has been a locally recognized poet for many years, sharing her work at readings and events, and is delighted to be publishing her first book. She has led a writing group since 1999 and is a member of a weekly poetry critique group with poet icon Fran Claggett-Holland. Her poetry has been published in the Redwood Writers poetry anthologies *Beyond Distance, And Yet* and *Crow*, in which she was an Award of Merit poet. Her work has been performed live by Off The Page Readers Theater.

Margaret is also an educator. She is inspired by the courage of people who are open to learning and making a difference in our world. When she was a single mother of three, Margaret went back to college and earned a master's degree in Psychology. She then trained to facilitate the MBA Interpersonal Dynamics course at Stanford Graduate School of Business. She has taught for over twenty years, most recently in the Organization Development Masters Program at Sonoma State University. Her latest love is leading women's retreats in the Grand Tetons.

Margaret is relentlessly curious, noticing the details of life—the tiniest shift of expression, surprise connections, and small mysteries—and is compelled to write her observations, allowing her reader to share the beauty, sorrow, and humor of this world through her poetry.

For her, writing is an opportunity to explore the workings of a complex and gorgeous world. Margaret arranges ideas, ingredients, words, and emotions into the offerings of her heart: a jar of jam, a basket of tomatoes, a carefully crafted poem.

margaretbarkley.com
margaretbarkley@sonic.net

CPSIA information can be obtained
at www.ICGtesting.com
Printed in the USA
LVHW092104280122
709443LV00005B/650

9 781646 625963